Dana

How to Store Shoes: Ideas, Tips & Tricks
- Illustrated guide and Practice -

Table of Contents

General Introduction

General Introduction

Choosing the right **shoe storage** for your home is not as easy as it seems.

The **ideal storage** allows you to have the shoes you use regularly at your fingertips, protect the pairs you wear more rarely, while keeping a **well-organized interior** . Taking the time to look for the best way to **store shoes effectively** is also to find the right solutions to keep your home **clean** without mess.

From the **simplest** storage (a floor-standing shelf) to the **most advanced** (a wardrobe entirely dedicated to shoes), solutions and ideas abound.

There are **many ways to organize and store shoes** everywhere in the house. With suitable furniture or DIY fabrications, you will discover all these ways of **organizing your shoes** .

Storage suitable for all situations (large family in a large house or single in a small studio), for **all budgets** and especially for all **types of shoes** .

Whether you prefer to **hide** and hide them or to **display them** proudly, you will find in this guide **cheap, functional, modular** and even **decorative solutions** for shoe storage.

Because there are as many solutions for **shoe storage as shoe** styles, browse this guide and find the best ideas.

Before you start

Before looking for the **best storage cabinet** and discover all the tips and ideas, the best thing to do to **simplify the storage of your shoes** is simply **to sort** .

The more you **limit the number of shoes** to put away, the more the organization will be **simple, fast and efficient** .

If you have a **limited budget** or live in a **small space** , it also saves space and money, without even having to start looking for your **shoe storage** !

Step 1: make an inventory

The first step, certainly the **most important** . Make an inventory of **all the shoes**you wish to store.

Will you wear them soon? Are these shoes damaged? Even if you decide to keep all these shoes, **an inventory** is always a useful step.

You may be able to realize that you finally have **less shoes** to put away than expected.

Step 2: give / sell

Do you have **too many shoes to put away** and you do not have enough room to install a piece of furniture with sufficient capacity?

Do a good job **giving the shoes** you no longer wear, or sell the unused pairs. This will allow you to put aside money to invest in a piece of furniture or accessories adapted to **store the shoes** you want to keep.

Step 3: Set aside

Some shoes are to keep but **to put aside** . We think of seasonal shoes, boots, summer shoes, ...

You can **put them aside** if you do not wear them in the next few months. Store these shoes in **plastic crates** , in a room where you have space (for example the garage, the laundry, ...).

No need to keep your winter shoes in the entrance in summer. Especially if you are looking for solutions or **ideas "space saving"** to store and organize your shoes. You will discover suitable accessories for storing seasonal shoes at the end of this guide.

Step 4: expose or conceal?

You will discover that some storage **conceal shoes** , while others " **expose** ". We can actually find lots of ideas to **showcase her best pairs of shoes** in the room, in the doorway, in the living room, ...

Choose the storage according to your desires. This is usually a matter of **personal preference** . Some people prefer the more aesthetic and "clean" appearance of **closed storage,** while others take advantage of shoes to decorate and stage their interior!

1 - How to choose the most suitable storage for your shoes?

The perfect solution for **storing shoes** is the one you will use every day, without any special effort!

Every situation is different, every home too. Each **shoe storage** must therefore be adapted.

Beyond the purely aesthetic and decorative aspect, the following points are **to be taken into consideration** during your research.

Storage stability

An **important aspect** to consider, especially for shoe racks without wall mounts. The **good stability** of the shoe cabinet is important if you do not want to transform your storage into a "Leaning Tower".

Modular storage furniture , which you can stack, is practical, but the **main disadvantage** is usually **lack of stability** .

The capacity of the shoe storage

Plan a storage or a piece of furniture **adapted to the number of shoes** to put away.

From **small** studio **furniture** to **large storage** for all the shoes of the family, you have the choice.

Easy to clean & maintain storage

It is important to **regularly wash the furniture** on which you store your shoes. Choose a **furniture easy to maintain** , in a **place easy to clean** .

The ability to customize and modulate storage

Modular storage space to store shoes and boots of different sizes

Some storage for shoes **seem practical** , but check that they are **well suited to the size** of your shoes (boots, high shoes, heel, ...). For this, we recommend **modular furniture** that you can customize easily.

The type of shoes to put away

Boots do not fit in the same way as summer sneakers. The ideal storage therefore adapts to **different types of shoes** .

The room in which to store shoes

Ideally, and if you have room, you can **organize and store** your shoes in **several places** .
In the entrance for example, you use the space available to store **only the shoes**that you use **most regularly** .
The other pairs of shoes are to be grouped in boxes to put them aside and put them in another room (the garage, a cupboard, under the bed in the room, ...)

2 - Where to store shoes?

Shoe storage in the entrance

The best way to store **shoes in the entrance** , if you have enough room, is to install a **bench with a** built- **in storage box** .

Un banc pratique pour le rangement des chaussures dans l'entrée

In addition to providing a **comfortable solution** to **put on and take off** easily, you have access to a convenient and dedicated storage space, which allows to group your shoes to avoid disorder.

Note that the **storage space** can be **closed** (safe)
or **open** (shelves under the bench).

Certainly the **most used and most popular** shoe
storage . However, be careful not to **clutter the
entrance** , which remains a place of passage and must
above all **remain functional** despite the many comings
and goings.

If you run out **of space** but still want a dedicated space
for **storing your shoes in the entrance** , install a piece
of furniture with drawers. It will serve as **a convenient
console** to store keys and all the things to take with you
before going out.

A fine piece of furniture that can store shoes in the entrance without taking up too much space

The storage of shoes in a dressing room

If you have the place, the budget and especially a **lot of shoes to put away** , you can provide a **dedicated dressing room** . Use a small, unused room or a large closet.

A room entirely dedicated to the storage of shoes: the dressing room for shoes

You can also add an **existing dressing room** with shelves or **wall storage** for the shoes. This **saves space** and does **not clutter the floor** .

A dressing area with a reserved area for storing shoes

The storage of shoes under the stairs

A **discreet, practical and functional solution** , which makes it possible to conceal the **shoes under the stairs** . Disadvantage, this arrangement usually requires a **custom installation** that can be expensive if you are not a handyman.

Practical, discreet and well thought out layout under the stairs
for shoe storage

To make yourself from a **sliding rail** , the space under
the stairs is transformed into a **clever storage for shoes** .

A sliding rail and a custom fit for storing shoes under the stairs

source https://bit.ly/2NCbJFr

The empty space **under the stairs** can also accommodate **open storage for shoes** , boots and sneakers.

Open storage for shoes under the stairs

The storage of shoes on the doors

The storage of the **shoes on the doors** do not have the best reputation. Generally **weak** , they can also **damage your doors** and **cause problems** to close them.

If **you lack space** , these storage spaces are yet **practical** !

It is recommended that you read **customer reviews** on e-commerce sites before buying a door storage model. Do not forget to **take the measurements** !

A metal storage, to hang on a door for hanging shoes

The storage of shoes in the room

A wardrobe entirely dedicated to the storage of shoes in the room

Under the bed, in a closet or even in a corner, there are different ways to store shoes in the room .

Stow the shoes in the room, behind a curtain

The curtain offers a simple and aesthetic solution to hide the shoes that are stored in the room

To store the shoes in the room, concealing them.

Store shoes in the bedroom, on open shelves

Use open shelves at the headboard to store and expose the shoes in the room

A **headboard to expose and store the shoes** in the room. **Easy to install** (with shelves as open shelves), but certainly **not the most practical solution** to access the shoes!

Store shoes in the room under the bed

Convenient for **small spaces** , and especially for storing shoes that you want to **put aside** , or those that are not in season.

Une housse de protection en tissu et en plastique permet de ranger et de protéger les chaussures sous le lit

A suitable storage cover helps to **protect the shoes** and slip them under your bed. A preferable solution for all **the shoes of season** , which you do not put regularly.

Clever, practical and discreet storage for sliding shoes under the bed (to be made with wooden boxes and wheels)

A **clever and discreet storage** to slip shoes under the bed, with wooden **boxes and wheels** .

A rigid transparent box to store and slide the shoes under the bed

There are also **rigid boxes on** transparent **wheels** . Practical to quickly see the **contents of the storage** and find the shoes that we seek quickly.

A practical and ingenious accessory on wheels to easily store shoes by sliding them under the bed

Practical **storage** accessories **on wheels** , for easy access to the **shoes under the bed** .

Storing shoes in a hallway

The storage of shoes in the hallway

Of **wall shelves open** metal on several levels to store **shoes in the entrance** , right next to the door.

For an apartment or house occupied by **a family** , each member can have **his own shelf** . Book
the **lowest** floors **for children** , they can access it more easily!

The storage of shoes in the garage

The storage of shoes in the garage allows to unclutter the space available in the house

If you have a garage, this is probably the most suitable room for storing and **storing seasonal shoes** , as well as **sneakers for the sport** .

The advantage of this piece to store your shoes is that you can bet on purely practical and functional solutions and **put aside the decorative aspect** .

The storage of shoes outside

A boot protector that stores shoes outside the house

Practical if you have **direct access to your garden** , this storage allows you to **wear the boots outside** to avoid getting dirty inside your home. This shelter also protects the **shoes from the rain** .

Shoe storage in nooks and crannies

A storage column for shoes, suitable for nooks and crannies in small spaces

Every inch counts ! The **nooks and crannies** of your home or apartment can turn into **storage for your shoes** . Generally **DIY ideas to make oneself** are the most suitable, because custom.

Shoe storage under the eaves

A custom-made shelf, under the eaves, to optimize the storage of shoes

The **attic and attic** , forgotten spaces with **good potential to store shoes** that are not used or that are worn less regularly. We can also transform these **lost spaces into a** custom **dressing room** to store shoes with heels.

3 - The different storage cabinets for shoes

There is as much **furniture to store shoes** as **shoe** styles .... Wooden, PVC, fabric, plastic, small or large, decorative or functional, ...

A piece of furniture for storing shoes, up to 24 pairs

The **appropriate shoe rack** meets your criteria and needs. **How many shoes** do you want to store, do you prefer an **open or closed storage** ?

Other criteria to consider when choosing a **shoe storage cabinet** ? Style, design, solidity, price, ...

Shoe bench

A practical bench for storing shoes in the entrance, with a comfortable cushion for shoes and shoes.

BUY : shoe bench https://amzn.to/30HwcfN

benefits of the shoe bench

o   it can be used to complete the layout of an entrance with other furniture and accessories (wall hooks for example).

o   generally available prices

o   many models available in all styles

- some benches are equipped with practical drawers

- easy to move

- takes up little space in a small entrance

- comfortable to put on / off easily

Shoe locker

A cloakroom locker for storing shoes

advantage of the shoe rack

○   aesthetic: cloakroom or industrial style

○   large storage capacity

disadvantage of the shoe rack

o takes up space

o bigger budget

for which room

o a grand entrance

Shoe shelves

A shelf for storing shoes

source https://www.ikea.com/fr/fr/

advantage of the shoe rack

o   choice between fixed or rolled shelves

o   choice of sizes and storage capacity

o   small shoe shelves can be installed in a cabinet or closet to maximize storage space

disadvantage of the shoe rack

o   unsightly

for which room

o   entry

o   bedroom

o   the dressing room

Telescopic shoe rack

A telescopic shelf for storing shoes. Unattractive, but very practical to store many shoes and have them at hand.

BUY : telescopic shoe storage Wenko

https://amzn.to/2ZwH8Q0

Modular shelf for storing shoes

Adjustable Shoe Storage Shelf, 2-6 Levels

Shoe rack with stand

A practical storage shelf for shoes, with 4 levels and supports

BUY : Harry Compactor shelf https://bit.ly/2Pl6igK

Shoe showcase

storage cabinet for shoes with a showcase. The good
decorative idea? Staging his best shoes under a glass bell!

source https://bit.ly/2UdnLGL

advantage of the shoe showcase

○ aesthetic

○ protects shoes from dust

disadvantage of the shoe showcase

- fragile

- not suitable for families with young children

for which room

- bedroom

- entry

- the living room

Shoe closet

A closet for storing shoes

advantage of the shoe closet

○   large storage capacity

disadvantage of the shoe closet

○ takes up space

○ custom installation

for which room

○ entry

○ bedroom

○ the dressing room

Wall shoe rack

Wall storage for shoes

advantage of the wall shoe range

- optimize space

- unclutters the floor

disadvantage of the wall shoe range

- request an installation with wall mounts

- not suitable for tenants

for which room

- entry

Storage of door shoes

A storage for the shoes to fix on the door

BUY : door shoe storage https://amzn.to/2L3y79a

advantage of storage of shoes on doors

o space saving

o practical and functional

inconvenience of storing shoes on doors

- lack of strength

- can damage the door

- unsightly

for which room

- all rooms in the house

Fine furniture for shoes

Fine furniture that does not clutter the space for storing shoes

advantage of fine furniture to store shoes

- limited space

- practical and functional

inconvenience of fine furniture for storing shoes

o   no

for which room

o   entry

Shoe cabinet

A storage box for shoes, with a padded cushion for a
comfortable and functional seat

BUY : <u>storage chest for shoes</u> <u>https://amzn.to/2ZyoqDA</u>

advantage of the shoe box

- o practical and functional

- o some chests are equipped with a comfortable seat

- o limited space

- o affordable price

disadvantage of the shoe box
- o limited storage space

for which room
- o entry

- o bedroom

Vertical shoe rack

A vertical shoe rack, which saves space, with a handle, easy to move

advantage of storage for vertical shoes

- o limited space

- o space-saving storage

- o can move easily

- o suitable for tenants

disadvantage of vertical shoe storage
- o limited storage space

for which room
- o entry

- o bedroom

Hanging Shoe Storage

A hanging storage for shoes, which can store shoes in a
wardrobe, dressing room or closet

BUY : <u>16-pocket hanging shoe rack Stuk IKEA</u>
<u>https://bit.ly/32e9zQC</u>

advantage of hanging storage for shoes

- o practical and space saving

- o affordable price

disadvantage of hanging storage for shoes

- o no

for which room

- o the dressing room

- o the cupboards

- o bedroom

Modular and stackable shoe storage

Stackable and modular storage for shoes

BUY : SongMix modular storage cubes

https://amzn.to/349wjCK

advantage of modular and stackable storage for shoes

- practical and flexible

- fits all spaces

- for all types of shoes

disadvantage of modular and stackable storage for shoes

- o lack of strength

for which room

- o entry

- o bedroom

- o the dressing room

- o the garage

Foldable shoe storage

A folding shelf to optimize the storage of shoes in small spaces. This shoe rack is also stackable.

BUY : GREJIG IKEA shoe rack https://bit.ly/2Ued0Uu

advantage of foldable storage for shoes

- practical and complementary

- little settle in a closet

- space saving

- affordable price

disadvantage of foldable storage for shoes

- limited storage space

for which room

- entry

- bedroom

- the dressing room

- the garage

the storage of shoes with mirror

Furniture with mirror for shoe storage

advantage of storage for shoes with mirror

- ○ practical and functional

disadvantage of storage for shoes with mirror

- higher price than a classic piece of furniture

for which room

- entry

Shoe cabinet

A simple and functional shoe cabinet with 2 lockers

BUY : Shoe cabinet 2 lockers Bissa IKEA

https://bit.ly/2LczYau

advantage of the shoe cabinet

- o hide shoes

- o store them easily

- o possibility to find a suitable model (storage capacity)

disadvantage of the shoe cabinet

- o no

for which room

- o entry

Shoe column

A column for storing shoes

advantage of the shoe column

- o optimize storage in small spaces

disadvantage of the shoe column

- o custom installation

for which room

- o the "lost" spaces

Horizontal shoe rail

A horizontal rail that attaches to the wall to optimize shoe storage

BUY : JME shoe rack https://amzn.to/2MKCrfs

advantage of the horizontal shoe rail

- o convenient

- o does not take up space

disadvantage of the horizontal shoe rail

- o asks to install fixtures in the wall

- o limited storage capacity

for which room

- o entry

Shoe rack

A simple grid to pose against the wall transforms into
practical storage and space saving for shoes with heels

advantage of the shoe rack

o cheap

o practice (moves easily)

o decorative storage

disadvantage of the shoe rack

- o   only for high heels

for which room

- o   entry

- o   bedroom

4 - DIY shoe storage

There are **hundreds of DIY ideas** to make yourself a **shoe storage** .

Home-made manufacturing makes it possible to imagine, design and install a **custom storage unit** , which corresponds to both the number of pairs to be stored, but also to the available space.

For starters, you can use objects or materials that you already have.

You can also buy everything you need to get started making a **storage for your shoes** .

You will find many inspirations on Pinterest. You can also find **tutorials** to get started.

The **most popular DIY** ideas are to use **PVC tubes** , make a **drawer on wheels**to slide under the bed or to make a **ladder or a tower** to store shoes.

Make DIY shoe storage with PVC tubes

DIY manufacture of shoe storage with PVC tubes

TUTO : leroymerlin.fr https://bit.ly/2NAcfUi

DIY manufacture of a storage for shoes to slide under the bed

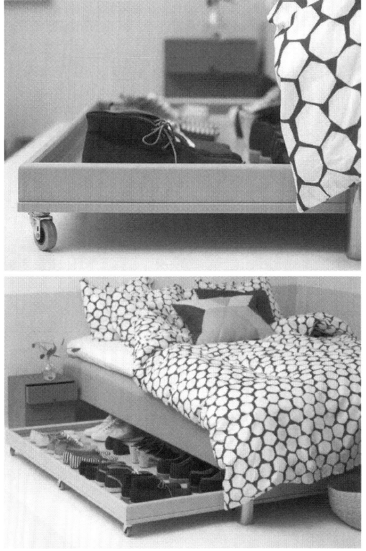

A storage for shoes to make yourself with accessories and IKEA furniture. Convenient, this shoe rack on wheels slips under the bed!

DIY manufacture of a tower for storing shoes

A shoe rack tower to manufacture oneself with ladders. DIY idea for shoe storage

TUTO : apairandasparediy.com https://bit.ly/2Lm25Xr

5 - Tips, ideas and tips for storing shoes

Separate shoes to store by collections

If you want to **store your shoes** in your closets and the space is limited, separate the shoes into **several collections** and find other **storage space** in your apartment or house.

Remember that the **ideal storage** for your shoes is scalable, and you do **not need**to store all your pairs in one place!

Enjoy **"lost" spaces** : under the bed, behind the doors, in the garage, in the guest room, ...

You may need to provide **several accessories or furniture** for storing shoes in these different rooms.

To **make it simple** , start with a **2 or 3-level shelf** in the entrance for the shoes you wear most often, and complete with **plastic boxes** for seasonal shoes, to put aside.

However, if you put shoes on the side, be sure to **clean them** before placing them in boxes or storage boxes. Also check if the **room is damp** , as this may damage the shoes.

Take action

Before buying a shoe cabinet, do not forget to **take the measurements** . The space you have, but also the **height of the shoes** to store in these furniture!

Choose the storage and accessories in relation to the type of shoes

The right storage also fits the **type of shoes** you want to store. For example, if you want to store **boots** , the ideal piece of furniture will have a **suitable height** .

Do not forget the protection of your shoes

The ideal storage should also provide **protection for your shoes** . Protect against dust in an apartment or house, against rain for storage in the garden, ...

To prevent the **boots from becoming deformed** , you can also hang them in a cupboard with **suitable hangers** .

A hanger with clips for storing boots, convenient to save space and prevent the boots from becoming deformed

BUY : hangers clips storage boots

https://amzn.to/32cpejb

This accessory, called the *Magic Shoe Rack,* makes it possible to **stack the shoes** on top of one another **without damaging them** , with the addition of a space- **saving appearance that is very practical** for small areas.

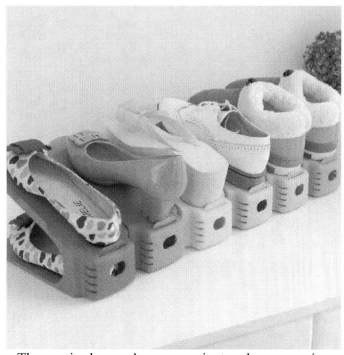

The magic shoe rack: a convenient and space-saving accessory to optimize shoe storage

BUY : magic shoe rack https://amzn.to/2PnAgR8